HOW TO...

DK

Soccer

A step-by-step guide to mastering the skills

LONDON, NEW YORK, MUNICH,
MELBOURNE, and DELHI

Project editor Alexander Cox
Project designer Sadie Thomas
US editor Margaret Parrish

Photographer Bill Ling
Production editor Sean Daly
Production controller Claire Pearson
Jacket designer Martin Wilson
Jacket editor Matilda Gollon
Publishing manager Bridget Giles
Art director Martin Wilson
Creative director Jane Bull
Category publisher Mary Ling

Consultant Alan Ackrell

First published in the United States in
2011 by DK Publishing
375 Hudson Street
New York, New York 10014

Copyright © 2011 Dorling Kindersley
Limited

11 12 13 14 15 10 9 8 7 6 5 4 3 2 1
180756–02/11

A catalog record for this book
is available from the Library of Congress.
ISBN: 978-0-7566-7581-3

Color reproduction by MDP, UK.
Printed and bound in China by Toppan.

**Discover more at
www.dk.com**

Contents

BEFORE KICKOFF

KEY SKILLS

WORLD OF SOCCER

"SOCCER can be played *anywhere,* by **anyone**, no matter your size, gender, age, or skill. Just **ENJOY** it! **"**

How to use this book...

This book contains lots of cool skills for you to learn. Each spread looks at a different soccer discipline, such as passing, and breaks it down into skills and drills.

The basic key skill is always shown in the orange box.

The movement of a player is always the same color as the player's uniform.

Skills are rated from easy (1) to hard (4).

The path of the ball is always an orange arrow.

Understanding the drills...

Some skills have drills that you can practice with your friends and teammates. Here's a key to help you understand them.

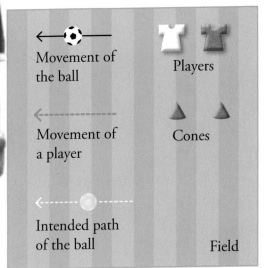

Movement of the ball

Players

Movement of a player

Cones

Intended path of the ball

Field

Are you ready to **master** the *beautiful game?* Let's go...

Before
KICKOFF

SOCCER is a fast and active sport. You will be running around, kicking, tackling, and scoring goals. But before you start with the ball, there's a lot to learn about the beautiful game, from the essential gear, to the field, to the basic rules. You'll also need to learn how to warm up your body so it's ready for action.

The gear

Before you start, let's have a look at what you will need to play soccer. Luckily, playing soccer is as simple as having a ball to kick. But when you start playing for a team or become a professional you will need all the right gear.

Shirts, shorts, and socks

The basic team uniform is matching shirts, shorts, and socks. Each has to be of a different color than the opposition's; otherwise, it will confuse the players. Professional teams have up to three different uniforms, so they don't clash with their opponent's uniform. These are known as home, away, and third uniform.

Numbers

The team's numbers used to run from 1–11, but, today, professional teams have squad numbers where players can choose their own numbers. Some players have high numbers, such as 88 or 99, on their shirts.

Soccer balls

There are lots of different types of ball out there:

Size 4

Circumference
25–26 in
(63.5–66 cm)

Size 5

Circumference
27–28 in
(68.5–71 cm)

Felt-covered
indoor ball.

SKILL BALL
A mini ball for skills and tricks

*GLOVES
The palm on each glove offers a gripping surface to help catch and hold the ball.*

The goalkeeper

A goalkeeper has to wear a different colored jersey from the outfield players, which shouldn't clash with the opposition or the match officials' jerseys. Goalkeepers can also wear different colored shorts; these can be padded on the side to offer protection when diving. Some goalkeepers wear tracksuit-style bottoms.

Shinpads

With feet kicking and swinging, your shins will get hit so you need to wear shinpads for protection, even when you are training. Some shinpads also have ankle protectors attached.

Shoes

Shoes protect your feet and help you grip the playing surface. There are three main types of soccer shoe: screw cleats, molded cleats, and the soccer sneaker.

SNEAKERS—these are most suited to hard ground or AstroTurf, and are usually worn during practice rather than during a match.

SCREW CLEATS—these are perfect for longer grass and give good grip on soft, slippery surfaces.

MOLDED CLEATS— these are best for the firmer field and offer good grip. They can be worn on artificial surfaces.

7

The field

You have your gear ready, so now all you need is somewhere to play. Soccer is played on a play area known as the soccer field. It is divided into two halves that have identical markings and goals. In competitive matches, the field has to meet certain rules and guidelines that control its shape, size, and markings.

Professional clubs and some local teams employ a groundskeeper to prepare and care for the field.

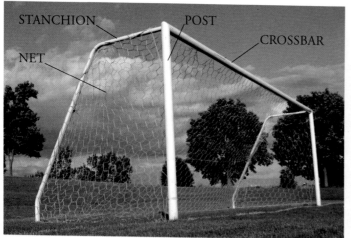

STANCHION   POST

NET   CROSSBAR

Know your goal
Soccer goals come in a variety of sizes, depending on the age range of the players. Goals in professional soccer are the biggest. They measure 24 ft (7.32 m) wide and 8 ft (2.44 m) from the goal line to the bottom of the crossbar.

Watching the match
To help you watch a soccer match, teams build seating around the field. Professional teams can have stadiums that can fit thousands of fans. Ellis Park Stadium in South Africa is home to the Orlando Pirates and can seat 62,500 spectators.

GOAL The goal sits in the middle of the goal line.

CORNER ARC

This quarter circle is where the ball must be placed to take a corner.

GOAL LINE

This is the end boundary of the field. If the ball crosses it a corner or goal kick is awarded.

CORNER FLAG

The flag shows where the touchline and the goal line meet.

PLAYING SURFACE

Most playing surfaces are grass, although they can be made from artificial materials such as AstroTurf.

PENALTY AREA

This is the area where the defending goalkeeper can handle the ball.

HALFWAY LINE

The halfway line divides the field into two identical halves. Teams defend one goal during the first half of the match, then switch ends and defend the other goal in the second half.

CENTER SPOT

This is where a kickoff happens, at the start of each half, and after a goal is scored.

CENTER CIRCLE

The center circle shows how far away defending players must stand at kickoff.

FIELD SIZE

The size of the field depends on the type of match and the age of the players. International fields have to be between 82 yd (75 m) and 70 yd (64 m) wide and 120 yd (110 m) and 109 yd (100 m) long.

TOUCHLINE

The touchline runs the length of the field. If the ball crosses it a throw-in is awarded to the team that didn't touch the ball last.

PENALTY ARC

The penalty arc is also known as the "D," and marks out how close players can stand when a penalty is being taken.

PENALTY SPOT

When an attacker is fouled inside the penalty area a penalty is awarded and taken from the penalty spot. It sits 12 yd (11 m) from the goal.

GOAL AREA

This is also known as the 6-yard box. Goal kicks are taken inside this area.

Team positions

A soccer team has 11 players, made up of one goalkeeper and 10 outfield players. The players are grouped into positions that play a specific role during the match.

GK GOALKEEPER

The goalkeeper is the last line of defense. He or she protects the goal and can use his or her hands to catch the ball.

AGILITY	★★★★★
POSITIONING	★★★★★
TACKLING	★★
HEADING	★
PASSING	★★★
SHOOTING	★
STAMINA	★★

Area of play on the field

★ **HANDLING**—A goalkeeper needs to catch and hold the ball confidently in lots of different situations.

Lev Yashin (USSR) Yashin played from 1949–1971 and was known as the "Black Spider." He possessed amazing agility and performed some super reflex saves.

D DEFENDER

A defender plays just in front of the goalkeeper and looks to stop the opposition from attacking and scoring.

AGILITY	★★
POSITIONING	★★★★★
TACKLING	★★★★★
HEADING	★★★★
PASSING	★★★
SHOOTING	★
STAMINA	★★★

Area of play on the field

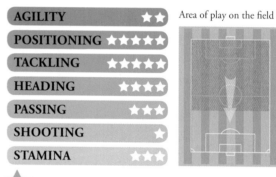

★ **MARKING**—A defender has to stay close and watch the opposition attackers so they don't score.

Franco Baresi (Italy) Baresi played from 1977–1997 and was an imposing and commanding defender. His positional skill made him very hard to get past.

> **"** *Which position should I play?*
> Not every player plays in the **SAME POSITION** all
> the time. Some players are *adaptable* and can play in
> **many positions**. Why not try out each position
> and see which you are best at? **"**

Ⓜ MIDFIELDER

A midfielder plays between the defense and
the attack. He or she supports the defense
and creates chances for the attack.

AGILITY	★★★
POSITIONING	★★★★
TACKLING	★★★
HEADING	★★
PASSING	★★★★★
SHOOTING	★★★
STAMINA	★★★★★

Area of play on the field

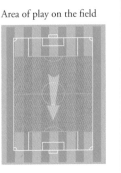

⭐ **VISION**—To perform a great pass, a
midfielder needs to see where his or her
teammates are headed.

Michel Platini (France) Platini played from 1972–
1987 and was a skillful midfielder. In addition to creating
many chances, he scored 41 international goals.

Ⓐ ATTACKER

An attacker's main role is to score goals.
He or she also needs to help out the
midfield and be good at creating chances.

AGILITY	★★★
POSITIONING	★★★★
TACKLING	★★
HEADING	★★★★
PASSING	★★★
SHOOTING	★★★★
STAMINA	★★★

Area of play on the field

⭐ **PACE**—An attacker with pace will scare
defenders and can create chances by running
past players.

George Weah (Liberia) Weah was a strong and
fast attacker and played from 1985–2007. He was the
first African to win the World Player of the Year award.

Laws of the game

To win a soccer match your team has to score more goals than the opposition. However, soccer isn't that simple, and like every sport or game it has a rulebook full of dos and don'ts that you have to learn.

WHO'S IN CHARGE?

The referee is the person in charge of a soccer match. He or she has several duties to make sure the match is played fairly.

Keep to the rules

The referee makes sure all the players on and off the field play within the rules of the game. He or she will control the game and stop play when it is required.

What's the time

It's the referee's job to keep track of time and make sure any delays are added on to the end of the game.

Safety first

The referee is responsible for the players' safety, so if a player is hurt the referee will allow him or her to have treatment.

Checklist

The referee makes sure the field, the goals, and the ball are good to use. He will also check that every player is wearing the correct uniform.

Helping out
Two assistant referees help out the referee. They offe an extra pair of eyes and keep track of the offside line. They patrol the touchline and use flags to signal to the referee.

It's a foul!

A yellow card is given for a bad foul or consistent foul play.

A player can also get a yellow card (also called a booking) for diving or arguing with the referee.

You will be shown a red card and sent from the field for a professional foul or violent conduct.

You will also be shown a red card if you commit a second yellow-card offense.

A game of two halves

A soccer match is played over two periods known as the first half and the second half. There is a short interval between the two halves known as halftime. A professional match is played over 90 minutes (45 minutes each half).

> **"** When the ball leaves the field of play the team that **DIDN'T TOUCH IT LAST** will kick, or throw the ball back into play. **"**

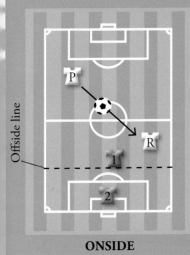

Goal!?

A goal is scored when the soccer ball fully crosses the goal line between the goal posts and below the crossbar. If a foul is committed before the ball crosses the line then the goal will be disallowed.

Handball!

Outfield players cannot use their hands while the ball is in play. A handball is given when an outfield player deliberately touches the ball with his or her arm or hand. Goalkeepers can only use their hands inside their team's penalty area.

OFFSIDE!

The offside rule makes sure teams don't try to gain an unfair advantage by having players "hang" around the opposition's goal. The offside rule has changed a lot over the last 150 years.

OFFSIDE RULE

When the ball is played forward by a player (P), the receiving teammate (R) must have at least two opposition players (1, 2) between him and the opponents' goal; otherwise, he is OFFSIDE.

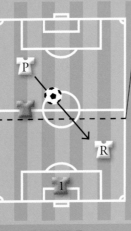

ONSIDE   **OFFSIDE**

ONSIDE!

The attacking player will *not* be considered offside if...

• he or she is **BEHIND** the ball when it is played forward.

• *the player is in an offside position*, but **DOES NOT RECEIVE** the ball and is not interfering with play.

• the ball is played *backward* off a **DEFENDING** player.

• the *attacking player* is in an offside position, but is **RUNNING** back onside and is not interfering with play.

Warm-up

It is important to warm up your body before you run around or kick a ball. It gets your muscles and brain ready to make those match-winning decisions.

OTHER WARM-UPS

- **Cone running**—Arrange cones in a pattern of your choice. Run from cone to cone, changing your running style. Maybe sprint, or run backward, or sidestep.
- **Catch and run**—Arrange your teammates in the team's formation and throw a ball around the team, swapping position with the person you have thrown the ball to.
- **Moving ball**—In a large coned area, pass the ball from player to player. You have to keep the ball moving. If it stops or leaves the area, everyone must perform five knee lifts.

AMOEBA TAG

Play in a large zone marked out by cones. Two players are "it" and form the amoeba tag chain. They hold hands and try to tag the other players, who once tagged, join the amoeba chain. The last player left untagged is the winner.

Untagged players must stay in the coned area; otherwise, they have to join the amoeba chain.

Watch out! When the amoeba chain is four players long it can break into two chains of two.

SKILLS SQUARE

This warm-up gives you a chance to practice your soccer actions. Make a square 11 yd (10 m) by 11 yd (10 m) and jog around the outside. As you run between the cones, perform a soccer action of your choice, such as a kick or a header.

Remember, the choice is yours. You can always perform the same action but with the other foot.

Why not rehearse your trapping skill or maybe a thigh control.

You can practice heading, jumping high, or even a diving lunge.

You can change your run, maybe try a sidestep, or even jog backward.

❝ A good warm-up gets your **MUSCLES** soft and flexible, which helps *prevent injury*. It's also a great time to **liven up** your MIND so you are ready to play. **❞**

MIRROR PAIRS

You need two players for this warm-up. Stand opposite your partner and choose who will be the leader first. The leader performs soccer moves of his or her choice, such as a kick or a header. The partner must perform the same move.

TACKLE TAG

Everyone has a ball in a coned area. You must keep control of your ball and try to kick another player's ball out of the zone. If your ball leaves the zone, you are out. You can have two active zones of tackle tag, so people don't have to sit out.

Key SKILLS

SOCCER isn't as simple as kicking a ball. Soccer involves lots of different skills you need to learn, from tackling, to heading, to passing and shooting. Different positions require different skills, and goalkeepers have their own set of special techniques to learn. There's a lot to master, so let's begin!

Can you kick it?

To reach the heights of soccer superstardom you have to start with the basics. And you don't get more basic than kicking the ball. Master this skill, and everything else will be a lot easier.

1 INSTEP KICK

The basic kick in soccer is known as the instep kick. The instep is where your shoelaces are on your shoes. It gives your kick plenty of control, power, and height.

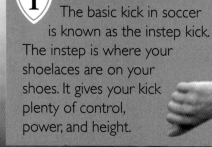

1. Place your standing foot next to the ball. Make sure it is pointing in the direction you want to kick the ball.

Place your foot so your toes are in line with the front of the ball. This will help you keep your kick low.

"Learning to KICK the ball is very important because most soccer skills involve KICKING.

DON'T USE YOUR TOES!

When you kick the ball, don't use your toes. This is a **BIG NO-NO**. Aside from making it hard to *control* the ball, a toe punt can damage your feet!

As you strike the ball, make sure you keep your head over the ball and point your toes.

LACES

2. Strike through the middle back of the ball with your shoelaces. Use your arms to balance.

STRIKE

3. After kicking the ball, let your striking foot follow through with the swing. Keep your body pointing at your target.

It is important to learn to strike the ball **CLEANLY** and **CORRECTLY**. And remember to *practice with both feet!*

Ball control

It is important to learn how to control the ball. From receiving a pass to moving with the ball, a good touch and control will give you time and space to pass and create chances.

Firm touch

In a match you will receive the ball and need to move away from defenders into space. Sometimes this will require a firm touch, which can protect the ball from defenders and allow you to change direction, while staying in control of the ball.

1

CUSHIONED TOUCH

Keep an eye on the ball as it comes toward you. Offer the inside of your foot to the ball and softly cushion it. The large surface area makes it easier for you to control the ball.

2 TRAP THE BALL

Another way to control a moving ball is to use the sole of your foot to trap it.

Don't raise your foot too high or the ball will skid underneath.

WATCH

1. Watch the ball and raise your trapping foot slightly, ready for the ball.

To keep the ball moving; you can trap, then gently roll the ball forward.

TRAP

2. Firmly place your trapping foot on the back top of the ball to control it.

3 THIGH CONTROL

This is similar to a cushioned touch, but you use your thigh to drop the ball down gently to your feet.

Keep an eye on the ball and offer your thigh to the dropping ball.

Make sure you keep your thigh soft, and cushion the ball on impact so it drops in front of you.

3 CHEST CONTROL

When the ball comes to you from a high pass, you will need to use your chest to control it. Make sure your arms are by your side and watch the flight of the ball. Offer your chest to the ball and bend your knees. This should help you to chest the ball softly so it drops just in front of you.

As the ball touches your shoelaces, flick your foot back to put spin on the ball.

4 LACES STOP

This skill is hard to master, so will take a lot of practice. As the ball comes to you in the air, offer the ball your shoelaces. When it strikes your laces, softly cushion the impact of the ball so it stops at your feet. Watch out—the ball can bounce off your foot in different directions.

Dribbling

When you run with the ball at your feet it is called dribbling. You can dribble into space or around players—both need a good touch, close control, and good balance.

Watch the pro
Lionel Messi is a master dribbler. He keeps the ball close to his feet, so he can change direction quickly and dart past defenders.

Running with the ball
The first rule of dribbling is to make sure you don't kick the ball too far in front of you. Keep the ball close to your feet so you can easily stop, change direction, and evade tackles.

"Remember to *keep your head up*. **DON'T** just look at the ball when you *dribble* because you might find that you have run off the field!**"**

BOTH FOOT DRIBBLE This practice improves your touch and close control with both feet.

RIGHT

LEFT

REWIND

1. Keep the ball close to your feet. Use the inside of your right foot to push the ball forward.

2. Now use the inside of your left foot to push the ball forward. Keep changing from right to left foot.

Once you have perfected dribbling forward, try it backward. Drag the ball from right to left foot and keep your balance.

2 DRIBBLE AROUND

This practice helps you control the ball while you move around obstacles. Set out three cones in a straight line. At first, make the cones quite far apart. Now use both feet to dribble around the cones.

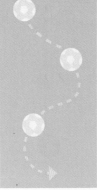

Keep the ball close to your feet and try to weave around the cones. Keep as close to the cones as you can.

GETTING GOOD
When you get better at dribbling around the cones, move the cones closer together, or set them out in a trickier pattern.

3 THE DUMMY

There are several tricks you can perform while you dribble the ball. The dummy is an effective and simple move that can fool defenders and help you dribble past them.

1. Dribble toward the defender in a straight line using both feet.

2. As you get close to the defender, drop your shoulder and pretend to turn to your right.

3. Step past the ball and then swerve the other way, using the outside of your left foot to take the ball with you.

Pass the ball!

Soccer is a team sport and it's made a lot easier when you pass the ball around. The idea is to let the ball do the work. To become a master passer you need good vision, touch, and control.

Possession play

When you pass the ball around your team it is called keeping possession. This is good because if you have possession of the ball, then the opposition can't attack!

If you pass the ball too hard your teammate won't reach it; too soft, and it will be blocked.

1 SIDE FOOT PASS

This is the basic and most used pass in soccer. You use the side of your foot because it is easier to aim the pass.

1. Place your standing foot next to the ball and point your toes toward your target.

POINT

2. Rotate your kicking foot so it is side on. Strike firmly through the middle of the ball.

PASS

3 THE THROUGH PASS

Sometimes it is best to pass the ball into space for teammates to run to. This type of pass can create a goal-scoring chance. It isn't easy to master, because you have to time it right, aim it, and get the power just right.

2 ACCURATE PASS

To help improve your passing you can try this easy drill. Start with the cones set wide and pass the ball through the cones to your teammate. Remember to practice with both feet. As you improve, reduce the distance between the cones and increase your distance from your teammate.

Keep an eye on the opposition—they will try to block your pass.

Your teammate will try to time his or her run, but you also have to pass at the right moment.

Watch the pro
One of the best passers of his generation is Xavi Hernandez. He possesses brilliant control, accuracy, and vision.

"VISION is really important when you want to make a *through pass*. Play with your **head up** and watch your teammates' movement. **"**

25

Crossing the ball

Crossing the ball from out wide can create some great goal-scoring chances. But, with defenders and a goalkeeper trying to get in the way, crossing is a hard skill to master.

The perfect cross

A cross is similar to a long pass. The main difference is you pass the ball from a wide position into the middle of the penalty area. Crossing is tricky because you are moving forward but trying to pass accurately to your side.

2 THE CUT BACK

A good way to create a goal-scoring chance is the cut back cross. When a wide player gets to the goal line they can accurately pass the ball back into the area along the ground. Also, there is no chance the receiving attacker will be offside.

Before you cross the ball, look up to see where your teammate is positioned.

1 SIMPLE CROSS

The most important part of a cross is your standing foot. Instead of it pointing forward, like on a normal kick, it should point in the direction of the cross. This helps you pivot and whip the ball into the middle.

Watch the pro

David Beckham of England is one of the best crossers in the world. He can judge weight, distance, and height perfectly, creating many goals.

3 BEATING THE FIRST DEFENDER

When you cross the ball, your first goal is to get your cross over the first defender who stands near the front post. This gives your teammates the chance to attack the ball and score a header or a volley.

Make sure the cut back cross has enough power to reach your teammate.

> **66** Always *remember* to **LOOK UP** before you cross. A great cross into space isn't as useful as *a cross to a teammate.* **99**

Clean Tackle

In a match, your team doesn't always have the ball, so you have to learn how to win the ball back. A good tackle requires concentration, commitment, and timing.

1 **BLOCK TACKLE**
A block tackle allows you to stay on your feet and win the ball back. It is important to watch the ball and block with strength.

1. Watch the ball and don't get distracted by the opposing player.

WATCH

2. At the right time, place your tackling foot into the path of the ball. Bend your knees to make your block more solid.

TIMING

3. Make sure you put your weight into the block tackle. If you don't, you may get injured.

BLOCK

Foul!
A good tackle can help your team win the ball back. However, a bad tackle can give away a free kick or even a penalty.

BAD TACKLE
Most bad tackles occur because the tackle is late. Timing is vital when you tackle. It is also important to be strong in the tackle, but if you are too aggressive you can be penalized.

2 SLIDING TACKLE

The opposition can attack at pace and you may have to run and slide to win the ball. For this move timing is really important.

Watch the pro
Serbia's Nemanja Vidić is a formidable defender. He has strength, pace, and can time his tackles perfectly.

You need to be certain that you can win the ball before you slide in. Get it wrong, and the attacker can knock the ball past you.

You can slide in and kick the ball out of the attacker's path. Or if you time it right, you can hook your foot around the ball.

Defending

Knowing how to tackle is only the start of learning how to defend. Stopping the opposition from scoring is also about working as a team and about concentration.

As a defender, you must keep one eye on the play, but also know where your opponents are.

2 DEFENSIVE LINE

To defend well, you have to defend as a team. You must concentrate on your area of the field and communicate with your teammates. Knowing where your fellow defenders are is very important.

Check you are in the correct position by looking along the defensive line. You don't want to stray too far out of position.

Marking

There are two main types of marking—man-to-man and zonal. Man-to-man marking is when you concentrate on marking a specific player and follow him or her around. Zonal marking is when you patrol an area of the field and mark any opponent who enters that zone.

3 *JOCKEYING*

Force an opponent into wide areas of the field by using the jockeying technique. The art of jockeying is not to commit to a tackle. Instead, close down the player to slow them down. Bend your knees and force them away from the goal.

1 *GOAL SIDE!*

The first rule of defending in any situation is making sure you are goal side of the attacker. You position your body between the attacker and your goal. This stops the attacker from having a clear run at the goal when they get the ball.

> **"** Defending is a lot easier if you are in the *correct position*. Being in the **right place** at the right time comes with **PRACTICE**. **"**

DEFENDING DRILL

This drill will help you **defend as a team**. You will need eight players split into two teams of four. The goal of the game is to **stop the opposing team from getting the ball into your end zone**. The team in possession of the ball (A) can pass the ball around, but can only score a point if they run the ball into the end zone. The defending team (D) must put pressure on the ball and mark the attacking players. You can intercept and block the ball, but *you are not allowed to slide tackle*. To make the drill harder, add an extra player to the attacking team, or create a goal to defend in the end zone.

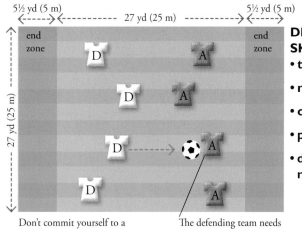

5½ yd (5 m) ⟷ ⟵ 27 yd (25 m) ⟶ 5½ yd (5 m)

27 yd (25 m)

end zone — D — A — end zone

Don't commit yourself to a tackle, because you will then be out of position.

The defending team needs to close down the player on the ball.

DRILL SKILLS
- **teamwork**
- **marking**
- **closing down**
- **positioning**
- **decision-making**

Heads up!

Soccer isn't just played on the ground using your feet—sometimes you have to use your head. You will need to master the skill of heading so you can deal with long, high kicks and crosses from out wide.

Practice makes perfect. Keep heading the ball and get a feel for it striking your forehead.

Standing tall
You don't need to be really tall to be a good header of the ball. Timing your jump and confidence play a big part in learning how to head the ball.

You use the center of your forehead because it is solid and hurts less when you head the ball.

1 SIMPLE HEADER
Learning how to head the ball comes from practice and confidence. First, hold the ball in your hands and throw it up in the air, just above head height. Aim to use the center of your forehead and strike through the center of the ball. Try to keep your eyes open.

Watch the pro
Tim Cahill of Australia is a world-class header of the ball. Although not tall, he can leap above defenders and scores many headed goals.

2 ***DEFENSIVE HEADER***
When defending you want to   head the ball high and far out of defense.

1. Stand with one foot slightly in front of the other and bend your knees. Watch the ball and move your forehead toward the ball.

2. Transfer power from your knees Head below the midline of the ball, sending it in an upward direction. Keep your hands by your side.

2 ***ATTACKING HEADER***
To score with a header you   have to use power and aim it low.

1. Have a solid stance, with one foot in front of the other. Keep your eyes on the ball and your hands by your sides.

2. Use your legs and neck to generate power and head above the midline of the ball, aiming it at the goalkeeper's feet.

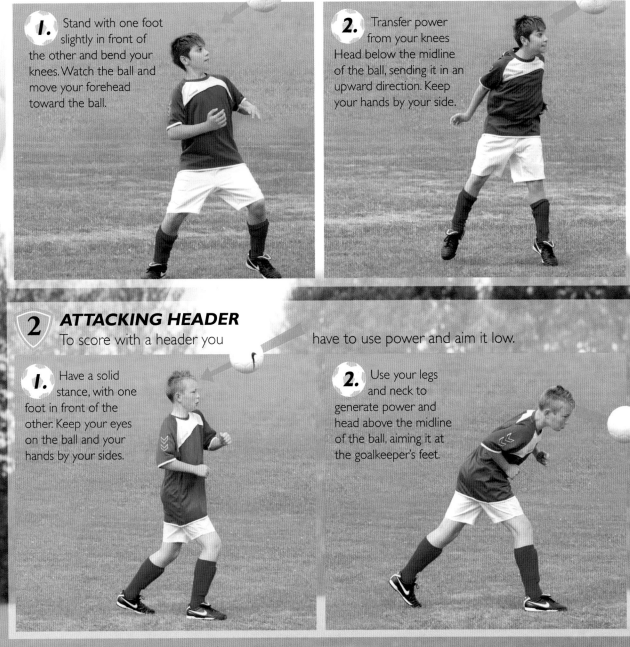

HEADING DRILL

This drill will **improve your heading confidence** and help you develop accuracy and control. This drill needs two players. One player is the heading player (H) the other is the thrower (T). Set up two goals 2 yd (2 m) apart. The thrower tosses the ball for the heading player to head. The heading player then chooses to perform a defensive header back to the thrower or a powerful attacking header through one of the goals. After a while, the players can swap duties.

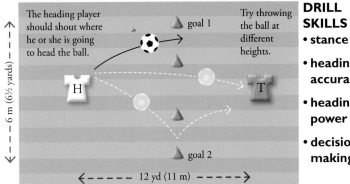

The heading player should shout where he or she is going to head the ball.

goal 1

Try throwing the ball at different heights.

6 m (6½ yards)

H   T

goal 2

← – – – – – 12 yd (11 m) – – – – – →

DRILL SKILLS
- **stance**
- **heading accuracy**
- **heading power**
- **decision-making**

Shooting

To win a soccer match you have to score more goals than the opposition. This is harder than it looks. A good goal scorer needs to be calm, accurate, and a quick thinker.

You decide!

When you receive the ball in a goal-scoring position, you will have to decide where to aim and how hard to strike the ball. Remember, the harder you strike the ball the harder it is to keep it on target.

1 BASIC SHOT

The basic shot is like a normal kick. With a big back lift, strike the ball with your shoelaces to generate power. Keep your head down and over the ball when striking, and concentrate where you want to aim your shot.

Remember not to lean back or swing your arm too far back, since you might strike the ball over the bar or wide of the goal.

You can aim for the corner nearest to you. The goalkeeper will be close to this area, so your shot will have to be very accurate and powerful.

Your striking leg should stop after the stab and not follow through.

2 THE CHIP

This crafty shot is great for getting the ball over an approaching goalkeeper. Go to strike the ball, then at the last minute use a stabbing action to get your foot under the ball.

Try to keep your shot low. A high shot is easier for the goalkeeper reach.

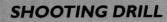

The best way to improve your shooting is to **PRACTICE**. You won't always be in the same position during a match, so this drill lets you shoot from different angles. You need three players for this drill. Set-up a goal and select a goalkeeper (G). You also need a passer (P) and an attacker (A). The passer starts with the ball and passes it to the attacker. The attacker then shoots at the goal. The passer then changes positions and passes from position 2 and then position 3. This changes the angle the attacker collects and shoots from. If you are getting good at shooting, try striking the ball first time or make the goal smaller, and remember to practice with both feet.

The passer can pass the ball along the ground or throw the ball into the air.

8 yd (7.23 m)

G

P

2

3

Start shooting close to the goal, and as you improve, shoot from farther away.

A

←————————— 18 yd (16.5 m) —————————→

DRILL SKILLS
- **ball control** • **decision-making** • **shooting accuracy**
- **shooting power** • **composure**

If you aim your shot across the goal your teammates have the chance to pounce on a rebound that may come off the goalkeeper or post.

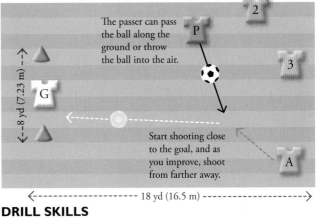

Watch the pro
Didier Drogba of the Ivory Coast is a great striker. He scores powerful strikes and well-aimed shots.

Attacking

Scoring a goal is a lot harder than it looks. To make it easier you have to attack as a team and make sure you pass and move.

Creating space
A lot of the time in a match you won't have the ball. Don't stand around and watch; instead, move around and create space for yourself and your teammates.

1 **ONE-TWO**
A simple and effective attacking play is the one-two pass. This involves two players passing the ball quickly between them and running into space. This move will create space in cramped areas of the field.

PASS

I. When close to a defender, pass the ball firmly into your teammate's feet.

MOVE

2. Run past your marker, as your teammate makes a first time pass into space.

3 **OFF THE BALL**
Running without the ball is an important skill for an attacker. You can run to through balls, create space for others, and lose your marker.

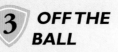

RECEIVE

3. If the move is played fast and is accurate you will get away from your marker.

PASS AND SPIN

This simple move allows you to create space and lose your marker with a quick pass and spin.

1. With your back to your opponents' goal, shield the ball from your marker and firmly pass the ball to a teammate.

2. Then turn with your head and spin around your marker, aiming to run into the space behind them.

3. Your teammate will then pass the ball around the defender into your path and you are off!

Try bending your run. When you are running off the ball, make sure you time it correctly. Run too early, and you will be offside.

ATTACKING DRILL

This drill will **improve your passing quality** and **decision-making**. The big decisions are when to pass and when to shoot. This drill is for six players—four are attackers and two play as defenders (D). Three of the attackers (A) begin in the start zone. One attacker acts as a receiver (R). The attackers pass the ball into the receiver, who passes it back to start off the attack. The attackers must now pass the ball around the play area and try to score a goal. The defenders must try to intercept the ball. As you improve, increase the number of defenders, or make the rule that an attacker can only take two touches before they must pass or shoot.

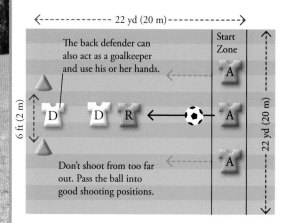

The back defender can also act as a goalkeeper and use his or her hands.

Don't shoot from too far out. Pass the ball into good shooting positions.

22 yd (20 m)

6 ft (2 m)

Start Zone

DRILL SKILLS
- passing • movement • ball control
- communication • decision-making

37

Safe hands

The last line of defense and one of the most important positions in the team is the goalkeeper. To be a goalkeeper you need good concentration skills, agility, and good eye-hand coordination.

1 CHEST CATCH
The chest catch allows you to catch and hold onto the ball securely.

1. Stand on your toes and bend your knees. Move your body in line with the flight of the ball.

WATCH

2. Offer your hands to the ball and use the W-hands grip to catch the ball securely.

CATCH

3. Bring your hands and arms around the ball to protect it and hold it close to your chest.

HOLD

Shot stopper
The first skill a goalkeeper must master is the use of his or her hands. The goalkeeper is the only player who can handle the ball, so must use it to his or her advantage. To be able to catch the ball cleanly you need good eye-hand coordination.

LOW STOP
Stopping a low shot looks easy, but you don't want the ball to slip through your legs. Watch the ball, and kneel down with your shin and foot creating a barrier. Spread your hands wide to help you catch and scoop the ball into your chest.

3 HIGH CATCH

As a goalkeeper you have the advantage of using your hands. This gives you extra height as you jump to catch the ball. Make sure you watch the ball and use both hands.

Keep an eye on the ball and catch it with both hands using the W-hands grip.

W-hands

Make sure your fingers and thumbs form a solid "W" shape behind the ball as you catch it. The W-hands grip gives you support and control when catching in any situation.

Try to keep your back as straight as possible. This gives you a strong foundation to catch the ball.

The raised knee makes your jump stable, so you aren't stretching too far. Also, try to point your toes down.

Super save

The ball won't always come straight at you, so you have to learn how to dive. Being able to dive means you can cover more of the goal and make it harder for the opposition to score.

Always try to use both hands, and concentrate on cleanly and firmly pushing the ball away with your palms.

DIVE AND CATCH

1. Have your hands ready and keep on your toes so you are ready to move your body sideways facing the ball.

READY

2 NARROW THE ANGLE

You need to make it as hard as possible for the attacker to score. When an attacker is one-on-one with you, narrowing the angle reduces the area of the goal the attacker can place his or her shot.

If you stay on your line the attacker can choose to aim his or her shot on either side of you, and it will be hard for you to reach.

3 PUSH AWAY DIVE

If you are at full stretch and can't catch the ball, you will have to push the ball away. It's important to push the ball away from the goal and out wide away from any opposition attackers who are looking to pounce on a rebound.

When you narrow the angle you can cover more of the goal, making it harder for the attacker to score.

When you dive to save the ball it is important to try to catch the ball. You'll get more confident with practice.

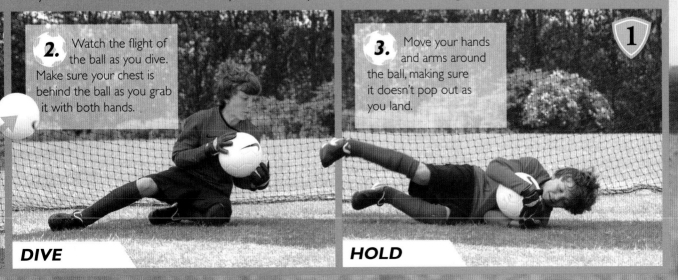

2. Watch the flight of the ball as you dive. Make sure your chest is behind the ball as you grab it with both hands.

3. Move your hands and arms around the ball, making sure it doesn't pop out as you land.

1

DIVE

HOLD

Distribution

You've dived, saved, and caught the ball. Now you need to pass the ball to one of your teammates so they can build an attack. Distribution is important because you don't want to throw the ball to an opponent!

66 **Be aware of the opposition. DON'T** just look at your *teammates' positions*, keep an eye on those pesky opponents who will *pounce* on a weak throw or kick! **99**

3 **HALF VOLLEY**
Another kick out is the half volley drop kick. It is similar to the drop kick, but you kick the ball just after it bounces. This kick can go really far, because the energy of your kick is increased by the energy of the bouncing ball.

DROP KICK The basic kick out is the drop kick, which allows you to kick the ball far up the field.

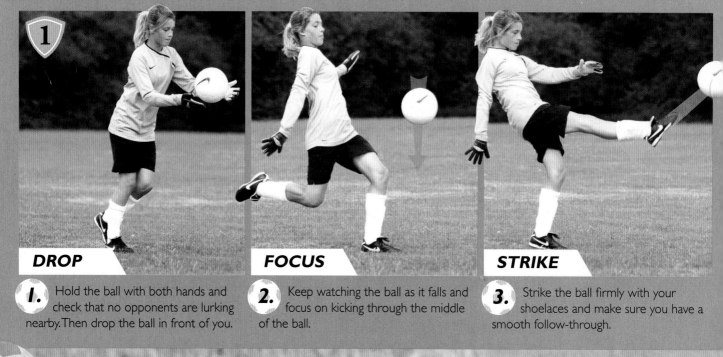

1

DROP

1. Hold the ball with both hands and check that no opponents are lurking nearby. Then drop the ball in front of you.

FOCUS

2. Keep watching the ball as it falls and focus on kicking through the middle of the ball.

STRIKE

3. Strike the ball firmly with your shoelaces and make sure you have a smooth follow-through.

Take a stride forward and aim with your free arm, then launch the ball toward your teammate. Don't throw it too high, since it will take a long time to reach your teammate and will be hard to control.

2 OVERARM THROW

The overarm throw allows you to get the ball to a teammate quickly and with some distance and accuracy. Be careful to keep an eye on the opposition and make sure they can't intercept it.

You can get more distance as you move forward, transferring energy from your legs.

2 THE ROLL OUT

This is one of the safest ways to pass the ball to your teammates. A roll out keeps the ball low and easy to control. It is also used over a short distance to an unmarked defender.

As you stride forward, use one hand to roll the ball toward your teammate. You can stabilize yourself with a bent knee.

During a match, you will have to keep moving to find space and offer your teammate an option to pass.

Teamwork

Soccer is a lot easier if you work as a team. Whether your team is attacking or defending everyone has a role to play, and if everyone puts in the effort you can win the game.

1 TRIANGLES
A simple and effective teamwork skill is passing in triangles. In a game situation, triangles give you two or more simple passing options, so you don't have to try a fancy trick or long pass.

The defender can only block one route, so you will always have an open pass to another teammate.

> **Always MOVE** around and find *space*. It's easier for your teammates to **PASS** to you if you aren't behind an opponent. **""**

Remember to use both feet to pass. This keeps your opponents guessing where you will pass and increases your passing options.

2 PASS AND MOVE

When you have the ball always look up to see where your teammates are running. Help each other by calling for the ball at the right time so you can receive a pass to your feet or into space in front of you.

TEAMWORK DRILL 10

This drill will get you **playing as a team**. The drill requires at least 10 players, five on each side. Each team needs to select a target man (T) and a wide player (W). The target man plays in the end zone, and the wide player operates at the side of the playing area. The three remaining players play inside the play area. The goal of the game is to pass the ball around the opposition team and get it to your target man. The target man has to control the ball inside the end zone to score a point. The team not in possession has to try to block and intercept the ball. The drill will be more challenging if a player can only take two touches before he or she must pass.

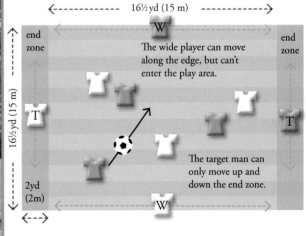

16½ yd (15 m)

16½ yd (15 m)

end zone

end zone

The wide player can move along the edge, but can't enter the play area.

T

T

The target man can only move up and down the end zone.

2 yd (2m)

DRILL SKILLS
• movement • passing accuracy • communication
• decision-making • first touch • marking

Playing as a team

An important part of teamwork is playing in formation. You may feel the desire to follow the ball, but it is vital for you to defend and attack in the area of the field that matches your position.

Play in position
In a formation everyone has a role to play. If everyone plays and stays in position your team will be hard to break down. But if you leave your position, gaps will open up for the opposition to run into.

TEAM FORMATIONS

4-4-2 This is a balanced formation that offers a solid defense, width, and attacking options.

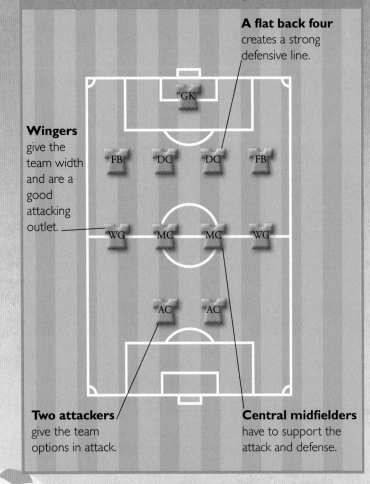

A flat back four creates a strong defensive line.

Wingers give the team width and are a good attacking outlet.

Two attackers give the team options in attack.

Central midfielders have to support the attack and defense.

4-3-3 This is an attacking formation and needs good support play between attack and defense.

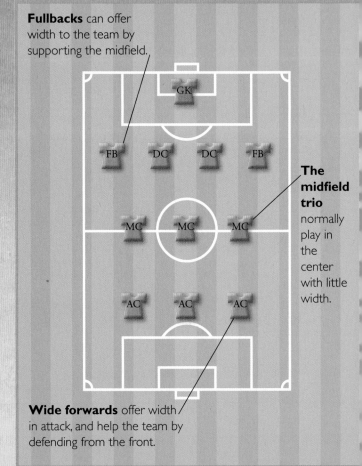

Fullbacks can offer width to the team by supporting the midfield.

The midfield trio normally play in the center with little width.

Wide forwards offer width in attack, and help the team by defending from the front.

POSITIONS KEY: **GK:** Goalkeeper • **FB:** Fullback • **DC:** Defense center • **SW:** Sweeper • **WB:** Wing back

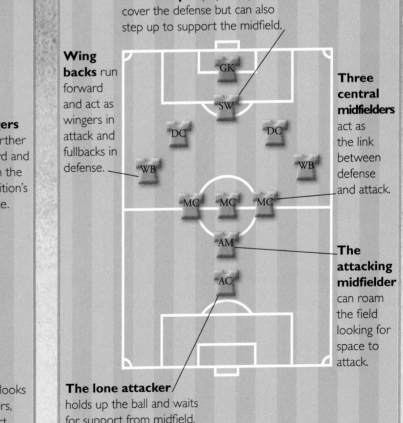

If you follow the ball you will leave space for the oppositon to exploit.

4-2-3-1 This modern formation is versatile, with good attacking options and a solid defense.

Two holding midfielders sit in front of the back four and move from side to side to give extra protection to the defense.

Wingers play farther forward and stretch the opposition's defense.

The attacking midfielder acts as a link between defense and attack.

The target man looks to play in the wingers, and midfield support.

GK
FB DC DC FB
DM DM
WG AM WG
AC

5-3-2 This formation has a strong defense, but with good support offers several attacking options.

The sweeper plays deeper to cover the defense but can also step up to support the midfield.

Wing backs run forward and act as wingers in attack and fullbacks in defense.

Three central midfielders act as the link between defense and attack.

The attacking midfielder can roam the field looking for space to attack.

The lone attacker holds up the ball and waits for support from midfield.

GK
SW
DC DC
WB WB
MC MC MC
AM
AC

DM: Defensive midfielder • **MC**: Midfield center • **AM**: Attacking midfielder • **WG**: Winger • **AC**: Attacker

3 FREE KICK
When a direct free kick is awarded and the ball is close enough to the opposition's goal, then you can have a shot. The opposition will line up a defensive wall 10 yd (9 m) away to try and block your shot.

Dead ball

Free kicks, penalties, and corners can create goal-scoring chances. They are all known as dead ball situations, because the ball is considered "dead" until it is thrown or kicked back into "open" play.

Corner kick
A corner is awarded to the attacking team when the ball crosses the goal line after touching a defending player. A corner kick must be kicked from within the corner arc. Corners are a good chance to score headed goals.

You can aim your free kick for the top corner behind the wall. The ball needs to be lifted over the wall and made to dip under the bar.

② PENALTY

A penalty is awarded when a defending player commits a foul inside the penalty area. Keep your penalty shot low and aim for a corner away from the diving goalkeeper.

The goalkeeper lines up the defensive wall so it protects the near post side of the goal. The tallest defender should stand at the post end of the wall.

An easier option is curling the ball around the wall. However, the goalkeeper normally stands on this side so you have to be very accurate.

① THROW-IN

A throw-in is awarded when the ball crosses the touchline. Make sure you throw the ball correctly or it will be awarded to the other team.

1. Keep both feet on the ground and behind the line. With both hands, bring the ball back behind your head.

BEHIND

2. Swing your arms forward and throw the ball. Make sure you release it above your eye level.

THROW

Tricks and turns

Soccer is easier to play when you keep things simple. But sometimes the only option is to perform a trick. Here are a few simple tricks that can get you looking good in no time.

To trick or not to trick
The art of the trick move in soccer is not how well you can perform it, but when you should perform it. Remember, it is better to choose an easier option, such as a simple pass, than to perform a fancy trick.

1 FAKE AND DRAG
This move helps you fool an opponent while quickly changing direction in a small space. It needs to be one fluid movement and will take some practice.

1. Go to perform a pass or shot, but at the last minute don't kick the ball.

FAKE

2. Instead, place your foot on top of the ball and in one movement drag it backward.

DRAG

3. With the same foot, touch the ball in a new direction, and away you go.

AWAY

2 STEP OVER
This skill is similar to the dummy (see page 23), but instead of dropping your shoulder, you step over the ball to change direction.

1. As you dribble, swerve your body to the left and move your foot as if you were going to touch the ball forward; remember to bend your knees.

This move was made famous by Johan Cruyff in the 1970s. It can be used to change direction quickly and put a defender off-balance.

1. Dribble with the ball and perform a fake pass. Make sure your standing foot is slightly in front of the ball.

2. After the fake pass, use the inside front of your kicking foot to flick the ball back through your legs.

3. Use your standing foot to turn and change direction, taking the ball with you.

2. Then, at the last minute, loop your leg in front and step over the ball.

3. As you plant your left leg (not too close to the ball), use it to push off and accelerate in the other direction, taking the ball with you.

World of SOCCER

SOCCER is played, watched, and loved all over the world, from the townships of Africa, to the parks of Europe, and the sandy beaches of South America. Soccer has had many great players, who have shown off their skills to millions of fans in the sport's big tournaments. Are you ready to join them?

Big kick around!

Soccer is a fast, exciting sport that requires lots of skill and is great to watch and play. The most amazing thing about soccer is that you can play it anywhere, with anyone, and even by yourself. All you need is a bit of space and a ball!

These children in East Timor enjoy kicking the ball around come rain or shine. Professional soccer can be played in any weather, even in the snow, when an orange ball is used.

Go for the goal

Soccer is played all around the globe, from your local park to the streets of Africa. If there's space for a goal and a round(ish) ball, then children will play. Here are a couple of games you can play with your friends.

STREET/PARK GAMES

Cup doubles (cubbies)

With one goal and a goalkeeper, players get into pairs and it's all-against-all. When a pair scores, they go through to the next round. The last pair is knocked out, and the next round begins.

Three and in

There's one goal and a goalkeeper. You can play this all-against-all, or together as a team. The first player to score a hat-trick switches with the goalkeeper.

Headers and volleys

This is a team game, again with one goal and a goalkeeper. The outfield players pass the ball around, but can only score with a header or a volley.

GRASS IS GREENER
Your local park is a great place to practice your soccer skills. Grass is the best surface for soccer because it has a solid, yet cushioned surface.

STREET SOCCER
Street soccer allows children of all backgrounds to play. The streets gave rise to Futsal and many professional players started out kicking a ball around their hometown streets.

Some children can't afford hi-tech shoes, so they play with what they have. Playing barefoot can improve your touch and control.

FREESTYLE PLAY

A great way to improve your touch and control is to juggle the ball—this is also known as keepy-uppy or freestyle soccer. The goal is to kick a ball up in the air lots of times in a row, without letting it bounce. You can kick it, or use your knee, head, shoulder, and even your neck. You just can't use your hands.

CONTROL
Freestyle players practice a lot. They need really good control and touch to keep the ball in the air.

Daniel de Vries from the Netherlands

BALANCE
Practicing your freestyle moves can help you improve your general playing skills. You need a lot of concentration, coordination, and balance to pull off fancy moves.

Rickard Sjolander from Sweden

FLAIR
Freestyle players compete in competitions, so they need lots of skills and creative tricks.

Jovanny Gonzalez from Mexico

Futsal

Futsal is a five-a-side version of soccer that started in 1930, in Montevideo, Uruguay. Brazil adapted and improved the sport and its popularity has spread around the globe. Futsal is a fast and exciting game that encourages close control, accurate passing, and quick thinking.

Each team is allowed one timeout per half to talk tactics.

As with regular soccer, players wear matching uniforms and shinpads.

Futsal skills

Futsal encourages players to improve and develop their technical skills. The smaller playing area and heavier ball means you have to be very accurate with everything you do. Your passing, movement, speed, decision-making, and first touch have to be exactly right before you can be a great Futsal player.

The only footwear allowed is canvas or soft leather sneakers with rubber soles.

The ball

The Futsal ball is smaller and heavier than a normal soccer ball. It doesn't bounce as high and encourages players to pass the ball along the ground.

Futsal ball   Soccer ball

" Futsal is *fast* and SKILLFUL and players touch the ball twice as often compared to other 5-a-side versions of soccer that use walled fields. "

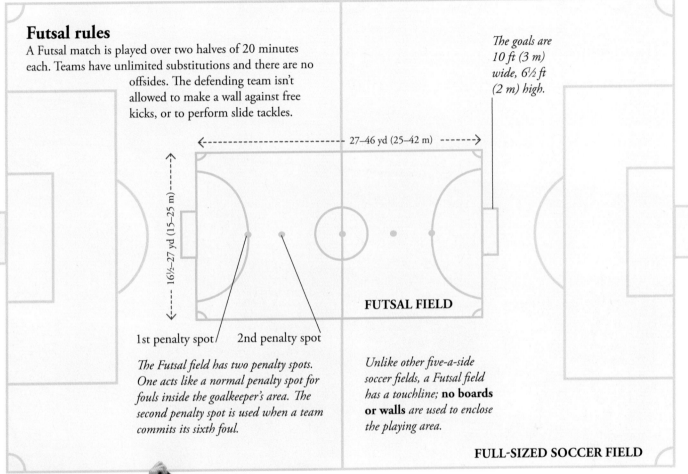

Futsal rules

A Futsal match is played over two halves of 20 minutes each. Teams have unlimited substitutions and there are no offsides. The defending team isn't allowed to make a wall against free kicks, or to perform slide tackles.

The goals are 10 ft (3 m) wide, 6½ ft (2 m) high.

27–46 yd (25–42 m)

16½–27 yd (15–25 m)

1st penalty spot   2nd penalty spot

FUTSAL FIELD

The Futsal field has two penalty spots. One acts like a normal penalty spot for fouls inside the goalkeeper's area. The second penalty spot is used when a team commits its sixth foul.

Unlike other five-a-side soccer fields, a Futsal field has a touchline; **no boards or walls** *are used to enclose the playing area.*

FULL-SIZED SOCCER FIELD

World champions!

There have been six Futsal World Cups—the first was held in Rotterdam, the Netherlands, in 1989. Only two countries have held the winners' trophy: Brazil (four times) and Spain (twice).

Amazing matches

The smaller size of the Futsal field allows it to be squeezed into unlikely places. This skyscraper Futsal field is in Toyko, Japan.

CSKA Moscow
(Russia)

AC Milan
(Italy)

Real Madrid
(Spain)

Bayern Munich
(Germany)

Soccer tournaments

The dream of every soccer fan and player, no matter where they live, is to play on the world stage, and at the world's greatest soccer tournaments.

The World Cup

This is one of the world's greatest sports tournaments. In soccer, it is the ultimate prize and all players dream of lifting the World Cup trophy one day.

The World Cup, played every four years, is hosted by a different country each time. The host country qualifies automatically, but every other country has to gain entry through regional qualification. The successful 32 teams play in eight groups of four teams. The top two teams from each group qualify for the knockout stages. Eventually, one team is crowned the World Champion!

The current World Cup trophy was designed by Italian Silvio Gazaniga for the 1974 World Cup in Germany. It is 14 in (36 cm) high and is made of 18-carat gold. It weighs 13½ lb (6.175 kg)— about the same as 15 cans of soda!

LA Galaxy
(United States)

Perth Glory
(Australia)

Júbilo Iwata
(Japan)

Mohun Bagan
(India)

Shamrock Rovers
(Republic of Ireland)

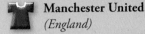

Manchester United
(England)

Liaoning Hongyun
(China)

Colo Colo
(Chile)

Going for gold

Soccer has been in every Olympics since 1900, except for 1932. The Olympics promotes amatuer competition, but allows professional soccer players to play as long as they are under 23 years of age.

Confederations cup

The Confederations Cup is played every four years and is used as a dress rehearsal for the World Cup. It is contested by the host country of the next World Cup, the current World Champion, as well as the champions of the six continental tournaments.

World Cup 2010 host South Africa held the FIFA Confederations Cup in 2009.

Continental tournaments

Each continent has an international tournament. Countries have to qualify for the tournament, and like the World Cup, the host country qualifies automatically. Here are the names of the six continental tournaments:

Asian Cup (Asia), **European Championships** (Europe), **Copa America** (South America), **African Cup of Nations** (Africa), **Gold Cup** (North America), **OFC Nations Cup** (Oceania)

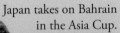

Japan takes on Bahrain in the Asia Cup.

Home leagues and soccer clubs

Every country has a league system in which teams compete over a season of fixtures to be crowned the league champion. Professional leagues normally contain 10–24 teams and a season can last up to 10 months.

> **❝** Most soccer clubs are based in a town or city. *Rivalries* occur when a town has **TWO** or more teams. **❞**

Al-Ahly
(Egypt)

Kaiser Chiefs
(South Africa)

Flamengo
(Brazil)

Boca Juniors
(Argentina)

59

Great players

The great debate of soccer is "Who was the best player?" You probably have your own favorite player, but here are a select few who have shown off their skills, won big matches, and lifted the world's greatest trophies.

GKP

Peter Schmeichel
DENMARK
(played 1981–2003)
Peter Schmeichel was a formidable barrier between the posts and for a goalkeeper scored an impressive 11 goals in his career, including one for Denmark against Belgium in 2000.

🇫🇮 **129** **1** **1**

DEF

Obdulio Varela
URUGUAY
(played 1936–1955)
Obdulio Varlea captained World-Cup-winning Uruguay in 1950. He was known as the "Black Chief" for his commanding presence in the heart of the team.

45 **9** **2**

DEF

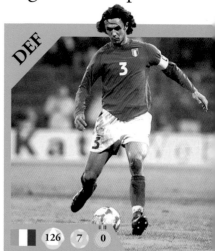

Paulo Maldini
ITALY
(played 1985–2009)
Paulo Maldini was known as "Il Capitano" and captained his country 74 times. He was a loyal player and played his whole career (25 seasons) for AC Milan.

126 **7** **0**

DEF

🏴󠁧󠁢󠁥󠁮󠁧󠁿 **108** **2** **1**

Bobby Moore
ENGLAND
(played 1958–1978)
Bobby Moore turned tackling into an art and was a great defender. He captained England to its only World Cup win in 1966.

DEF

Franz Beckenbauer
GERMANY
(played 1964–1983)
Known as "Der Kaiser" (The Emperor), Franz Beckenbauer played in three World Cups for West Germany and never finished lower than third place.

103 **14** **2**

MID

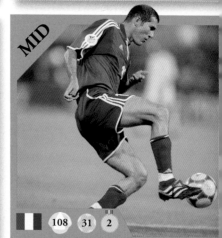

Zinadine Zidane
FRANCE
(played 1988–2006)
Zinadine Zidane is one of the most skillful players in history, and has had his trademark spin turn named after him.

108 **31** **2**

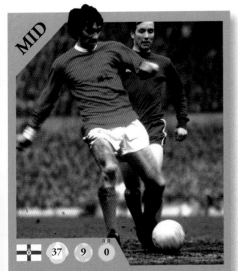

MID

MID

ATT

🏴 37 9 0

George Best
NORTHERN IRELAND
(played 1963–1984)
George Best was one of the greatest players never to have played in an international tournament. As a winger for Manchester United, he won many accolades, including the European Cup.

🏳️ 48 33 0

Johan Cruyff
THE NETHERLANDS
(played 1964–1984)
Johan Cruyff was known for his masterful technique. He was part of the skillful Dutch team of the 1970s that invented the term "total soccer."

🏳️ 91 34 1

Diego Maradona
ARGENTINA
(played 1976–1997)
Maradona was a skillful dribbler and has scored one of the greatest World Cup goals ever. He also scored a handball goal (known as the "Hand of God") in the quarter finals of the 1986 World Cup.

ATT

🇺🇸 275 158 2

Mia Hamm
UNITED STATES
(played 1989–2004)
Mia Hamm is the greatest female soccer player ever to have played the game, and has the title of the top international goal scorer of all time, male or female, with 158 goals.

Pelé
BRAZIL
(played 1956–1977)
Considered the greatest soccer talent ever, Pelé (real name Edison Arantes do Nascimento) is the top scorer of all time, with over 1,000 professional goals.

ATT

🇧🇷 92 77 3

Glossary

Adaptable A soccer player who is able to play in more than one position.

Agility The ability to be graceful, quick, and flexible. Used to note how much a goalkeeper can dive.

Along the ground When the ball is passed or shot so it moves near the ground. It is easier to pass and control a ball that is played along the ground.

AstroTurf A grasslike artificial surface that is used as the playing surface on a field. It was named after the Astrodome arena in Houston, Texas, where it was first used.

Away team The visiting team that is not playing at its own field or stadium.

Away uniform The team's uniform that is worn when it is playing away and its home uniform is similar to the opposition's.

Calling for the ball The act of communication performed by players when they are receiving or chasing the ball. This lets their teammates know they are after the ball.

Close down When a defending player moves toward the opposition player who has the ball, and makes it hard for him or her to dribble or pass.

Composure The ability to act in a calm and quick fashion under pressure. Normally used to describe an attacker's ability to convert goal-scoring chances.

Cover When a midfielder or attacker supports the defense and fills any space an attacking defender has left open.

Crossbar Part of the goal that sits on and joins the two goal posts.

Cushioned touch A soft touch that stops a fast-moving ball. Normally used to describe a player's first touch.

Dead ball When the ball is kicked out of play, or a foul is committed, the ball is termed out of play and "dead." Free kicks, corners, goal kicks, and penalties are all examples of a dead-ball kick.

Formation The pattern and shape a team of players make when they play a match.

Front post The goal post that is nearest to the ball when it is kicked or thrown toward the goal.

Home team The team that is playing at its own field or stadium.

Home uniform The team's primary uniform that is worn when the team plays a match at its home field, or if it plays away against a team with a different-colored uniform.

Hosts The country or team that holds and organizes a tournament in its territory or stadium.

Instep The top part of the foot, where the shoelaces are tied. Simple kicks are performed with the instep.

Interfering with play A term used to figure out if a player is offside. If a player plays an active role in an attacking move, then he or she is interfering with play.

Knockout stages The rounds of a tournament that see teams play one match, and only the winning team progresses to the next round. Losing teams are knocked out until only two teams remain, and a final is played to determine the winner.

Match officials The referee, assistant referees, and the fourth official, who are in charge of the soccer match.

On target A term used to describe a shot that is going to go into the goal.

One-on-one A situation where an attacking player has only the goalkeeper to get past in order to score a goal.

Open play When the ball is passed around during a match and does not leave the field of play.

Opposition The team of players that you are playing a match against.

Pass When a ball is deliberately and successfully moved from one teammate to another.

Post The upright part of a goal, which supports the crossbar.

Pressure on the ball When one or more defending players moves toward an attacking player in possession of the ball, in order to limit his passing or shooting options.

Professional foul A foul that is committed by the last defender on an attacking player who would otherwise have been through on goal.

Rebound When a shot, header, or kick bounces off a player or post into the path of another player.

Shield the ball The act of protecting the ball from an opponent by placing your body between the opponent and the ball.

Shot A kick that is deliberately aimed at the goal with the intention of scoring a goal.

Sidestep A style of running sideways in a skipping fashion.

Stance How the body is positioned when you perform a soccer action.

Stanchion A support bar on a goal between the crossbar and post, which also helps to hold up the net.

KNOW THE CALL!

Standing foot The foot that remains in contact with the ground when you perform a kick.

Striking foot The foot that makes contact with the ball when you perform a kick.

Tackle A move that successfully and fairly wins the ball back from an opponent in possession of the ball.

Tactics A series of moves, ideas, and positions that influence how a team plays during a match.

Teammates Players who play on the same team.

Third uniform The team's third choice uniform; it is worn when the team plays a match away against a team with the same color uniform.

Total soccer A soccer philosophy coined in the 1970s to describe the soccer style of the Dutch national team. It includes the idea of players being able to play in many positions.

Violent conduct An aggressive and deliberate act of violence against a player, such as a kick or punch.

Volley A shot that is performed before the soccer ball bounces.

World player of the year An annual award given to the best player in the world. This is voted on by international teams' coaches and captains.

SWITCH IT!
Shouted when there is an opportunity for the ball to be passed quickly from one side of the field to the other.

TIME!
Shouted when the receiving player has space and time to control the ball and look at his options.

IF IN DOUBT, KICK IT OUT!
Used to make sure defenders don't hold on to the ball too long, or try a fancy move. Instead, defenders are encouraged to kick the ball off the field to allow the team to regroup.

MAN ON!
Shouted to warn a teammate that an opponent is hot on his heels and he doesn't have much time to control the ball.

PUSH UP!
Shouted by a defender or goalkeeper to make sure the defensive players all move up.

LOOK FOR THE OVERLAP!
Shouted to wide players in possession of the ball to play the overlap tactic. This is when a fullback runs forward past the winger. The ball can then be passed forward to the fullback.

Index

Alan Ackrell has been an English FA qualified coach for over 30 years. He devises and teaches courses for aspiring coaches and also specializes in youth soccer. Alan holds an U.E.F.A "A" License and is the soccer development officer for Hertfordshire County FA. He is also a lifelong Arsenal supporter.

Acknowledgments

Dorling Kindersley would like to thank Carrie Love and Lorrie Mack for their editorial assistance; Lauren Rosier and Poppy Joslin for their design help; Rob Nunn for picture-research assistance; the Cavendish School and Richard Woodard for the use of their playing fields, and the fantastic models: Mark Berg, Thomas Carson, Sam Bailey, Justin Fields, Jack Stevens, Jordan Rogers, Richa Patel, Stephanie Collier, Georgia Zambardi, Phoebe Boyd, Katie Kay, and Savannah Francis-Christie.

Picture credits

The publisher would like to thank the following for their kind permission to reproduce their photographs:

(Key: a-above; b-below/bottom; c-center; f-far; l-left; r-right; t-top)

Alamy Images: Stephan Zirwes / fStop 9. Corbis: Matthew Ashton / AMA 8tr, 57br, 58-59; Bettmann 60bl; Nic Bothma / EPA 55br, 55cr, 55cra, 59tr; Philippe Caron / Sygma 52-53; Mario Cruz / EPA 56l; DPA / EPA 61br; Greg Fiume 61cl; Hulton-Deutsch Collection 10bl; Tibor Illyes / EPA 57bl; Frank Kleefeldt / DPA / EPA 61tr; Christian Liewig / Tempsport 10br; David Madison 10-11; Ocean 4-5, 12l; Omega Fotocronache / DPA / EPA 60cra; Olivier Prevosto / TempSport 60crb; Gerard Rancinan / Pierre Perrin / Sygma 11bl; Christine Schneider / Zefa 6bl; Kris Timken / Blend Images 16-17; David Turnley 55cl; Werek / DPA / EPA 60cb; Heinz Wieseler / DPA / EPA 61tc. Dorling Kindersley: Mitre 7tc. Dreamstime.com: Elnur Amikishiyev 7fcrb; Chris Hill 8cl; Ruben Paz 13cl; Phartisan 7bc, 7br. fotolia: Damelio 7fcr; Jose Manuel Gelpi 7cla; IvicaNS 7ftl, 7tl. Getty Images: AFP Photo / Adam Jan 59bl; AFP Photo / Greg Wood 32br; AFP Photo / HO 60ca; AFP Photo / Javier Soriano 58clb; AFP Photo / Liu Jin 25bl; AFP Photo / Michael Urban 27tl; Bongarts 56cr; Andre Chaco / FotoArena / LatinContent 12cr; Thomas Eisenhuth / Bongarts 56tl; Gallo Images / Danita Delimont 54-55; Gallo Images / Max Paddler 8b; Richard Heathcote 13tr; Anja Heinemann / Bongarts 7ftr; Chris McGrath 22tr; Tertius Pickard / Gallo Images 11br; Popperfoto 60cla; Riser / Siri Stafford 55tl; Quinn Rooney / FIFA 35br; Clive Rose 29tr; Taxi / Anthony Marsland 59cr; Bob Thomas 61tl; Tobias Titz 48ca. Clare Marshall: Nike 7cb.

Jacket images: Front: iStockphoto.com: Zentilia b.

All other images © Dorling Kindersley
For further information see: www.dkimages.com